Voices from Young Writers: A Collection of Poetry

Voices From Young Writers:
A Collection Of Poetry

Edited by Allison Jones

First published in Great Britain in 2009 by:

 Young**Writers**

Young Writers
Remus House
Coltsfoot Drive
Peterborough
PE2 9JX
Telephone: 01733 890066
Website: www.youngwriters.co.uk

All Rights Reserved
Book Design by Spencer Hart & Tim Christian
© Copyright Contributors 2009
SB ISBN 978-1-84924-347-6

Foreword

Young Writers was established in 1991 to nurture creativity in our children and young adults, to give them an interest in poetry and an outlet to express themselves. Seeing their work in print will encourage them to keep writing as they grow, and become our poets of tomorrow.

Selecting the poems has been challenging and immensely rewarding. The effort and imagination invested by these young writers makes their poems a pleasure to enjoy reading time and time again.

Contents

Georgia Hooley (10) 1	Lauren Parfit (8) 42
Charlotte Atkinson (11) 2	Chelsea Sacha Stagg (11) 43
Falak Khan (7) 3	Mishika Mahendra Parwani (11) 44
Niamh Randall (9) 4	Charlotte Spiller (11) 45
Victoria Brittain (10) 5	Louise Jillan MacKinnon (8) 46
Katie Greenaway (11) 6	Karen McAllister (10) 47
Naseema Khalique (12) 7	Cameron Harper (11) 48
Rebecca Smith (10) 8	Gemma Mae Burke (7) 49
Harry Jones (10) 9	Bethany Hare (9) 50
Federica Picariello (17) 10	Sam Tait (9) 51
Jenna Buxton (11) 11	Jordane Julia Cummins (11) 52
Emma Pearcey (15) 12	Catherine Bradley (12) 53
Maddy Foy (9) 13	Georgina Bennett (12) 54
Katie Reynolds (9) 14	Annabelle Fowler (10) 55
Isabelle Moss (10) 15	Georgie Hope Gregory (11) 56
Pia Johnson (11) 16	Heather Clarke (12) 57
Phoebe Ashmore (12) 17	Thasin Choudhury (11) 58
Miranda Kuyk (10) 18	Leah Rees (12) 59
Jabbar Fazal (11) 19	Dylan Chambers (7) 60
Devon Nicks (12) 20	Sambhav Gupta 61
Autumn Binns (13) 21	Umara Iqbal (8) 62
Eliza Maria Scott Thomas (9) 22	Uzo Anthony-Uzoeto (10) 63
Saeran Rowland (14) 23	Holly Louise Longthorn (9) 64
Lochlann O'Higgins (8) 24	Jacob Rimmer (8) 65
Amanpreet Flora (12) 25	Robert Staines (13) 66
Donna-May Player (12) 26	Mikhail Adetunji (7) 67
Hazeq Khalid (14) 27	Anna Everest (12) 68
Hayley Smith (10) 28	Ben Cross (11) 69
Bethan Slocombe (10) 29	Ziad Al-Dujaili (8) 70
Tammy Griffin (13) 30	Rhiannon Wilkins (9) 71
Emma Jayne Galley (11) 31	Alice Marriott (9) 72
Jessica Roberts (11) 32	Racquel Quinn (8) 73
Tayyib Mohammad (12) 33	Molly McKenna (9) 74
Evie-May Kilby-Tyre (11) 34	Aina Ahmed (10) 75
Esmee Bates (8) 35	Paige Murphy (9) 76
Sian Cummins (9) 36	Naila Ali (11) 77
Mohammed Umar Khan (12) 37	Yusuf Mohamed Makaran (10) 78
Esther Oguntona (12) 38	Sabeela Shamraiz (10) 79
Ellie Ogier (13) 39	Iveren Yongo (13) 80
Jack Morley-Brown (12) 40	Alicia Roe (9) 81
Rebekkah Barry (10) 41	

Birralee International School, Norway
Joanna Elisabeth Lee (12) 82
Conrad Johannes Bali (12) 83
Shreeram Ro Akerkar (12) 84
Rebecca Gjaetrvan Saether (12) 85
Mats Langseth (12) 86

Cardinal Allen School, Fleetwood
Phoebe Miller (12) 87

Crossgates Primary School, Llandrindod Wells
Sally Price (10) 88
Gareth Owen (9) 89
Morgan Margetts (9) 90
Lauren Jones (8) 91
Siobhan Margaret Patten (8) 92
Carys Powell (8) 93
Ben Jackaman (9) 94
Minnie Alder (8) 95
Tom Dunt (8) 96
William Dunt (8) 97
Abraham Berriman (9) 98
Emily Pugh (9) 99
Chloe Lisa Jones (9) 100
Jessica Layton (9) 101
Josef Dunn (9) 102
Tyler Owens (9) 103

Longstone Primary School, Ahoghill
Andrew Bowyer (9) 104
Tara McClure (9) 105
Hollie Dickey (9) 106
Jack McMillen (9) 107
Scott Harris (11) 108
Joshua McKay (11) 109
Jessica McMillen (11) 110
Ruth McNeilly (11) 111
Christopher McKay (9) 112

Newall Green High School, Wythenshawe
Rebecca Wilding (12) 113
Natalie Greenwood (12) 114

Simone Glindon (12) 115
Brooke Hirst (13) 116

Queensborough First School, Queensborough
Chloe Joyce (8) 117
Nicholas Post (7) 118
Jack Batt 119
Ocea Ratcliff (7) 120

Regent's Park School, Shirley
Melissa Pontes (13) 121

St Joseph's Catholic Primary School, Rugeley
Nathanial Humphries (10) 122
Keir John Scarlett (10) 123

The Rutland College, Oakham
Jack Seton (16) 124
Rachael Pick 125
Gary McDonald (16) 126
Rory McDade (10) 127
Francesca Hepplewhite (16) 128
James Harrison (17) 129
Rebecca Fisher (17) 130
Fiona Crew (17) 131
Charlotte Bourne 132
Tom Bell (16) 133

Trafalgar Junior School, Twickenham
Tristan Robayo Price (11) 134

Two Waters Primary School, Hemel Hempstead
William Nicholls (9) 135
Hasan Ali (9) 136
Megan Stockford (9) 137
Edward Langley (9) 138
Madeleine Greeves (10) 139
Findlay Hardcastle (9) 140
Charles Monk (9) 141
Bryn Holmes (9) 142
Leah Howey (9) 143
Charlotte Howey (9) 144
Frankie Toseland (9) 145

Aaron Wharfe (9) 146
William Howe (9) 147
Robbie McIvor (10) 148
Leon Axell-Gee (8) 149
Myers Witter (7) 150
Joseph Alexander Metcalf (7) 151
Jack Cannings (7) 152
Lydia Victoria Bradley (8) 153
Jessica Finnamore (8) 154
Jessica Pritchard (7) 155
Edward Shaw (7) 156
Matthew Say (7) 157
Millie Shaw (10) 158
Rory Howe (10) 159
Hannah Bartrip (10) 160
Harry Owen (10) 161
Hannah Baldwin (10) 162
Gail Miller (10) 163
Lucas Rogers (10) &
Nicholas Roel-Adams (11) 164
Abigail Morris (11) 165
Angela Chu (10) 166
Yasmine Hughes (10) 167
Amy Wordsworth (10) 168
George Morley (10) 169
Olivia Reeve (10) 170
Anna Bennett (10) 171
Jacob Jenkins (10) 172
Paige Ann Ford (9) 173
Tommy Walter (9) 174
Fynn Archibald (9) 175
Rutwik Mudholkar (8) 176

Ysgol Uwchradd Llanfyllin, Powys
George Andrews (12) 177
Matt Wheeler (11) 178
Ryan Risdon (11) 179
Charlotte Turner (12) 180
Shannon Pearce (11) 181

The Poems

I Am Lost And Alone

The fog followed me like honey stuck to a bee.
The wind cried out like it was trapped and needed help.
The faces in the sky glared at me like I was bait.
The dead trees swayed like they were going to grab me
And suck me into Hell.

I was lost
The voices of the graves whispered like the stream dripping.
The rain fell like dead souls returning.
The moon shone like a ghost growling.
The clouds hummed like a tramp wishing.
I was lost and alone.

Georgia Hooley (10)

Books

Books sit on the shelves
They sit all by themselves.

What you see is a pile of dirty old books
Long ago they lost their looks.

No one looked at or in their mind reflected
Nobody cares about them, they are neglected.

The pages are brown and torn
Not like the day they were born.

Charlotte Atkinson (11)

Dream

My dream was about a fish,
This was my best wish.
I love to dream
About a colourful ice cream.
I had a dream about a polar bear
Flying with me in the air.
I dream every day about a bright rainbow
But having a nightmare - oh no!

Falak Khan (7)

Under The Sea

Sitting on the rocks thinking what's in the water
Seaweed covering my toes
The nice breeze going through my hair.

Think . . . think . . . think . . .

Mermaids and angelfish
Yummy on my dish
Sharks and whales
They all tell tales.

Think . . . think . . . think . . .

The end of my day
As I walk to my house
It's getting dark as I walk down the street
Dogs and puppies go past me.

Think . . . think . . . think . . .

Having my tea, laughing at myself
For I think of all the funny stuff I said
Of thinking of the tale-telling sharks.

Think . . . think . . . think.

Niamh Randall (9)

I Miss 2008

I miss 2008
It was when I learnt to rollerblade,
Played with my dog Jade,
Rode on an amazing horse
And played football of course.

I miss 2008
It was when I learnt to ice skate,
Played with a wonderful mate,
Flew a beautiful kite
And stayed up to midnight.
Bye-bye 2008.

Victoria Brittain (10)

Oh No, What Shall We Do?

'Right PE time,' goes the teacher,
Oh no, what shall we do?
Dizzy Lizzie's forgotten her trainers,
Oh no, what shall we do?
Jolly Jack's lost his shorts,
Oh no, what shall we do?
Clever Chloe's got in a fight
With Dom and Tom,
Oh no, what shall we do?
Loopy Lucy is jumping off the walls,
Oh no, what shall we do?
Karate Katie's kicking silly Sam,
Oh no, what shall we do?
The teacher's given in,
Oh no, what shall we do?
All the kids shout and rave,
Teacher's too stressed to run today.
Oh no, I know what we will do . . .
Maths!

Katie Greenaway (11)

Candy Land

The candyfloss sky mounted high
Sugar-coated birds fly by
Long chocolate rivers flow slow
Dropping down white marshmallow snow.

Tall cookie buildings stand there
Hard toffee roads lead nowhere
Chocolate chip stars dotted
And ice cream houses spotted.

The lollipops sun bright and round
Haribo animals don't make a sound
Sweet sherbet paints a perfect sunset
This is a place I won't forget.

Naseema Khalique (12)

Register

'Right class quiet, quiet, it's time for the register.
Well, we need to do the register so we know who's here Claire.
Yes, I know we haven't started the register yet Jeffery, but don't worry, we're about to.
Oh no, where's the register gone?
Ben don't be silly, a monster hasn't taken it
Hang on a minute where has our class snail gone?
Daniel put it back in its tank and come and sit on the carpet
Ah good morning Mrs Bourly.
Well, that's great that your knickers fit now but I need to do the register so I'll speak to you later.
Daniel the snail!
Well, Michelle, I will do the register when we can actually find it.
Mrs Bouly, you're back are you?
Yes, I know your knickers fit now, you've already told me, but can you come back later?
Oh Daniel, where is the snail?
Well you had it last so you should know where it is.
What's that Katie?
You can see its head popping out of Daniel's pocket? Ah yes, I see it now as well.
Right Daniel, take the snail out of your pocket, put it back in its tank and come to the carpet.
Good boy.
Yes Ben, I know we haven't done the register . . . yet!'

Rebecca Smith (10)

Robot Warriors

Bish bash bosh
Clink clank clonk
Go the robot warriors
To protect their front

Some with powerful arms
And with powerful strength
Some with powerful attack
And some with powerful defence

Bish bash bosh
Clink clank clonk
Go the robot warriors
No more to protect their front

They have done their job
And a job well done
Those brave machines
All and one.

Harry Jones (10)

From Year To Year

Dear friend,
With me I'll take you
From every old year
To every New Year.
You are the treasure box
Of the happiness I've got
The good, the bad,
It's all now gone
But you are still here
Me and you, we have
And we will, many dreams
Together fulfil
And at the end of every
Year, I'll be wishing
For you to be here, as
I do every New Year.
Dear friend,
There's nothing I want
From last year, other than
The friendship we share
It's so dear -
You are the living proof
Of last year,
My memory of every year
My dear and precious
Friend.

Federica Picariello (17)

The Sea

I hear the water swirling around me,
Huge waves climb above me and crash down on the rocky shore.
Rain starts to fall and thunders down into the deep black sea,
Flying down, a bird is swallowed, gone from my sight like a flash
leaving no trace.

It roars up again, crawling high up into the sky,
And once again it crashes down with fury, devouring the stony ground
around me!
The white horses whinny ferociously
Riding the cruel rough waves.
The vast bottomless expanse of deep, black, harsh water
Stretches out far, far away.

My eyes water from the evil wind,
Icy sprays of salt spear at my chapped lips.
Dark clouds storm over my head
And the once blue sky vanishes from sight.

I plunge into this heartless sea
Waiting for the cold to grasp me
And it does.

Suddenly I find myself in a peaceful underworld
Away from treacherous world above me.
I stare in disbelief at the corals shining pink and orange
in the calm gentle water.
Magical fish dance elegantly in front of me, glittering in the bright light.

Jenna Buxton (11)

Inspiration

Have you ever gotten lost
In a book?
As you turn the pages
You immerse yourself
In the strange and wonderful lands
That fill your mind and make you
Forget about the worries of every day life.

Your mind full of fantasy
And magic, your imagination
Drifts and soars, flying away
To new worlds you created and, inspired,
You write them down.
Thoughts, feelings, pictures
Of places and people that come from you.
Mind far away, it guides the pen,
Weaving a tapestry of dreams.

Emma Pearcey (15)

A Winter's Tail

Getting coats on, Louis jumping all around,
Hats, gloves and socks for warm ears, hands and feet.
Look out the window, see frost on the ground
Check pockets, make sure we've got Louis' treats.

Just be careful of the road, 'Louis stay!'
'Good boy Louis' yum, getting his first treat.
Then into the field, Louis knows the way
Many walk this way, wonder who we'll meet?

The fields are covered in blankets of white
Louis dashing around this way and that.
Everything is such a wonderful sight
Everyone laughs at Dad's warm woolly hat.

Louis runs and runs soon we hear a splash!
What's that he can hear? Loud rustling sound.
Look, there Louis goes in such a wild dash,
There's the rabbit, off he goes with a bound.

Get back in the warm, give Louis some meat
We're all very tired, come on, let's rest.
'It's very cold, ' Mum says, 'turn up the heat'
'We enjoyed that,' I said, 'It was the best!'

Maddy Foy (9)

My Precious Friend

My precious friend never does lie
My precious friend has been there from the start
My precious friend is really caring
My precious friend kisses me goodnight
My precious friend can't catch me when I fall
But she is still my precious friend.

Katie Reynolds (9)

My Friend The Snowman

Wake up in the morning first thing that I see
Ha, can it really be?
Yippee! It's snow, oh I really have to go.
There will not be a moment that's dull
Because my day will be jam-packed full.
Soon we are walking along the path
That led to the park where we will use our sled
There are many marks in the snow
So anyone will know where we are about to go.
Soon we will all be making snowmen
And then they melt, but they're still my friend!

Isabelle Moss (10)

My Summary Of The Sound Of Music

S eventh of August our opening night
O smonds were our team,
'U s lot better behave yourself,' Russ would always scream
N ew friends we all have made
D ays were full of fun,

O xford Street, Covent Garden and Palladium!
F rank the director's notes were such a pleasure,

M eeting up with Andrew Lloyd Webber
U nbelievable applause to treasure!
S ad now it's all come to an end
I' ll miss you all, you're all my friends . . .
C an I say I feel privileged to a part of the team, I've loved every minute I have lived the dream.

Pia Johnson (11)

Time

As I sit beside my friends
I know I waste good time.
I know when I waste time
In lessons I don't like.
Why waste time on history
When I want to talk about
Time and the future?

You can't draw out time
From a bank down the road.
It happens when it happens
You can't change that
But why not make it better?

Time for this, time for that.
You want it all to spend with your friends.
No history or maths, just time and future.

Time is a wonderful thing to spend how you wish
To do your parents a favour or see your friends.
I want more time to spend watching a cloud on a hill
You may think I'm wasting time but I don't waste my life away.

Phoebe Ashmore (12)

My Favourite Things

If I had a world of my own, I'd make it recognisable, a world of my own.
The clouds would be as soft as lambs' wool,
The skies a deep blue velvet
And the ground would be nothing but pretty, purple duvets.
Stars would be patches of glitter on a black lace sky,
The glistening sun would sing,
Packages of coloured silk flowing in the fountains,
Sheets of delicate beads would billow at every doorway,
Golden buttercups and scarlet fuchsias would whistle in the breeze
Filling the world with a whispering hum.
The highest quality pearls twinkling in every tree,
Purple water filling the brooks running through the gentle green forest,
Rainbow feathers falling instead of hail, covering the ground with a lovely blanket.
If I had a world of my own, I'd make it recognisable, a world of my own.

Miranda Kuyk (10)

Early Extinction

Think about it . . .
The innocent snow tiger petrified of the poachers,
The desperate whales suffering from rubbish in the polluted sea,
The sweet animals' habitats destroyed by the vicious hunters.

Think about it . . .
The white fluffy polar bears dying,
The horrible enemies hunting,
The snow-white ice collapsing.

Think about it . . .
The innocent seals suffering for leather,
The yummy food vanishing due to selfish hunters,
The seals dying by poisonous oil in the deep blue ocean.

Jabbar Fazal (11)

Dog And Arty Fun!

Go dogs go!
Dogs are like my God
They are so cool and fun
You walk them in all weathers like the sun.
Go dogs go!
Go art go!
Let's go on to art,
Have you ever heard of the program called Smart?
I love art, it's the best,
I drew a picture, it was better than the rest.
Go art go!
Dogs are awesome!
Art can be gruesome!
Go art go!
Go dogs go!

Devon Nicks (12)

Love

Love is not something to be interpreted
Love is real
Love is something not to be missed
Never to be forgotten
Love is something to be embraced, never to be pushed to one side
Love is to be gracefully used
Never is love to be played as a card

Love can pick you up in a minute but can drop you down in a second
Love makes the world go round but it also makes it crumble
Love is like a human, two-faced but pretty to the eye.
Love is joyful when it's loved but painful when it is broken.
Love makes us happy, love makes us sad but love is not really all that bad.

Autumn Binns (13)

Winter

Jack Frost comes out, all is white
Be careful not to get frostbite!
Wrap up warm on these cold days
It will be a long time before we see the sun rays.
Look out for Santa on Christmas Eve
Mince pies and presents and lovely treats!
A carrot or two for Rudolph
Some cookies and milk for Santa.
A scrumptious turkey,
I can't wait till Christmas, can you?

Eliza Maria Scott Thomas (9)

The Theatre

Where can your heart soar higher than everything
Even higher than the moon?
Can you think of what causes fire to rage inside you
Warmer than the resilient sun?

Where can another world come so alive
Where nothing is as it seems?
Can you imagine a life so much like ours
But so different and new?

There is such a place
Where the crowd roar with joy
Or cry with such sorrow
And cheer when good prevails.

I know of such a place
So magical it's hard to tell
The difference from reality and fiction
A place simply called The Theatre.

Saeran Rowland (14)

Cool School No Rules

I go to a school where there is no rule,
For lunch we have sweets and no meat.

At lessons we play, no spelling all day,
We play football in class and never do maths.

The teacher doesn't mind that this poem doesn't rhyme,
She is happy we are free like a bird in the tree.

Lochlann O'Higgins (8)

My Brother!

My brother is kind of small
Although he likes to play football.
Most of the time he plays cricket,
He loves it when he hits the wicket.

My brother is great at maths,
He likes the food in the cafe.
He sits at home all day drawing
And when he goes to bed he can't stop snoring.

So what else can you ask from a brother?
You know very well he gets it from his mother!
So don't go and say that yours is the best
Because in the end mine will have the hairy chest!

Amanpreet Flora (12)

My Favourite Animals

Dolphins in the glittery sea
Looking gracefully as can be
Splashing, gliding, swimming
In the giant sea.

Tigers living in Africa
Not having to go so far
To look for these animals
Just look on the Internet for pictures.

Horses in the stable
Not needing TV cable
To keep them busy
All they need is a field
To roam around all day.

Koalas live in Australia
Climbing in the trees
Climbing, climbing higher
As high as high can be.

Donna-May Player (12)

Elation

There will be a day where you will experience great elation
Overwhelmed with anxiety
Every depth, breadth and height of your heart will soon jump with joy
Friends, families, foes will congratulate
The inevitable will soon come
It will, with patience
That surge of happiness through your veins
Oneself should believe
That there will be a day.

Hazeq Khalid (14)

The Cat

My furry cat with ginormous eyes sat on my hairy mat outside.
He clawed the mat with scissor-like paws.
His whiskers twitched as he sniffed the air.
He sneaked around without a care.
A scuttering rat quickly raced by
He dived across in the starry sky
He saw a spiky shadow zoom by.

Hayley Smith (10)

Seasons Of Fun

Spring has sprung,
Time for fun.
Taking a walk with my mum and dad,
Seeing daffodils flowering makes me glad.
Riding my bike through the mud
Getting dirty as children should.

Hip hip hooray! Summer is here,
Only the rain to fear.
Splashing about in a swimming pool,
Swimming around keeps me cool.
Me and my family going away,
Going on beaches to play.

Brown crunchy leaves, it is autumn today,
Taking my dog to the park to play.
Nice cooked dinner, steaming hot,
Lovely vegetables I have got.
Morning crisp and cold,
Putting my warmer coat on, I was told.

Dancing glittering snowflakes,
Icy snowy lakes.
Christmas trees the pretty lights,
The whole town is really bright.
Here it is Christmas Day
With my new toys I will play.

Bethan Slocombe (10)

My Birthday

I woke up in the morning
Windy as usual
Went downstairs but no one there!
Where could they be?

I went back upstairs into my room
But still no one there.
I wondered where they could be.

So I got dressed, had my breakfast turned on the TV and . . .
'Happy birthday,' they all screamed at me!

Tammy Griffin (13)

My Dog

George my dog is quite the best
He's slim and fluffy
Better than the rest.

George my dog is quite a sniffer
Sniffing all day
He sniffs in the grass and on the path
Sniffing all day to find his way.

George my dog is quite a player
Playing all the time
He plays in the garden
Hiding and finding.

George my dog is quite a barker
Barking at the gate
He barks at the post lady
He is great!
I love my dog George.

Emma Jayne Galley (11)

Christmas Presents

Christmas time is full of fun
Getting presents from everyone.
The Christmas tree sparkles,
The lights twinkle bright.
But it's what's underneath
That's my favourite sight!

I stroke them and prod them
To see what they are.
Oh I wish it was Christmas
I can't wait that far.

Christmas Day comes
I crash through the door.
Give me my presents
I can't wait anymore!

Jessica Roberts (11)

The Eagle

There is an eagle, what a nice bird
I watched it swerve in the air like as if it was in a herd.
It was staring at a turtle
The eagle was purple.

It came swooshing down
Through the town
It was close to the ground
The turtle headed for the sea which looked like it was crowded.

The eagle sat on a piece of wood
But that would do no good.
It had to get down and swoosh across the sea
And that's what it did, as he got closer he smiled with glee.

The turtle ducked under the waves
The distance between the eagle and the turtle got shorter.
The eagle grabbed the turtle by its shell
And flew up into the sky and the let go and the turtle fell.

The eagle followed it and took it to his nest
He had worked his best
He fed it to his babies
Who were going to become ladies.

This was the best day
He couldn't have anything else to say.
He looked down and saw a sheep
Then closed his eyes and went to sleep.

Tayyib Mohammad (12)

If I Could Be A Princess

If I could be a princess
A princess of a land
I would be called princess Evie
And be beautiful and grand.
I'd wake up every morning as happy as could be,
I'd hope a prince would be outside, waiting there for me.
And when the day was over, a banquet would be held,
If a villager was invited, my they would be proud.
And outside the castle, a villager I was
Hoping that I could be a princess, instead of a villager for once.

Evie-May Kilby-Tyre (11)

The Butterfly

Gracefully gliding through the sky
That's my favourite thing, the butterfly.
When the caterpillars start to eat
The life cycle begins to repeat.
Now let's start from number one
When the caterpillar's life has only begun.
Carrying on from number two
The poor caterpillar has nothing to do.
Let's skip to the cocoon
The butterfly will be arriving very soon.
The butterfly has now appeared
But the caterpillar seems to have disappeared.
Now the life cycle has come to an end
We have to say goodbye to my friend.
The life cycle will start again
From April to August we will see my favourite thing again.

Esmee Bates (8)

All About Me

Hannah Montana is my favourite star,
Strumming away on her favourite guitar.
I love animals, dogs are the best,
Nanny's dog Shay with his big white chest.
I like school maths and art are great,
I like eating healthy fruit on my plate.
I like wearing trousers, trackies and tops,
I really like spending and going to the shops.
My favourite colours are purple, pink and gold,
I love the sunshine and hate the cold.

Sian Cummins (9)

Stop Smoking

Smoking can kill
It can fill you with no good
It can burst your lungs
And rot your tongue.

You will get addicted
Thinking you're not affected
When you start coughing
That's a sign to stop smoking!

You are trying to be cool
But you look like a fool
You're acting smart
But you really aren't.

It makes your nails rotten
People think you should be forgotten.
Your lungs will turn black like the storm in the ocean
That is a sign of caution!

Inside it would not be nice
Because smoking has taken its time
So that you will die
Without saying goodbye.

Listen to the message
It's telling your mind
It's killing you inside.

Mohammed Umar Khan (12)

Just Beyond The Sunset

Just beyond the sunset
Someone waits for me,
Just beyond the sunset
Lies my destiny.
Where the purple mountain
Lies in deep serenity,
There I'll find the treasure.

Just beyond the sunset
Waits someone so fair,
Just beyond the sunset
All alone they wait there.
Their hair is golden
The colour of the sand,
Their eyes sparkle in the night
Like diamonds in your hands.

Just beyond the sunset
Lies a home for me,
Where the world is peaceful
Like a paradise should be.
Just beyond the sunset
Some day is where you'll find me.

Esther Oguntona (12)

Swimming

The whistle blows, we're under starter's orders,
The judges are stood ready in their corners
Timekeepers wait with their stopwatches
Everyone eagerly waits and watches.

Judges check zero is on the clocks
Second whistle blows and up onto the blocks.
We dive neatly into the pool
The water on our bodies is cool.

It's one of the important gala dates
Surrounded everywhere by teammates.
All eyes are on me
I'm representing my club GSC.

Everyone is loudly cheering
The end of my race is nearing.
I keep swimming and swimming
My hard work has been rewarded by winning.

Ellie Ogier (13)

On My Way To School I Saw . . .

On my way to school I saw a cheetah
It was a clever cheetah
It was a cunning clever cheetah
It was a colourful cunning clever cheetah
It was a crazy colourful cunning clever cheetah
It was a contagious crazy colourful cunning clever cheetah
And it chased me!

Jack Morley-Brown (12)

Stars

During the day the stars hide away
During the night, they shine so bright.
The stars are there to help old grandfather moon
Bright up the sky just after noon.
After the sun leaves the sky,
The stars jump out winking their eye.
Once the night comes to an end,
The dad star is happy, he was going round the bend!
The wisest star Ned,
Had his most brilliant idea, let's all go to bed!
It's like this every night
If you see a star remember, they're bright!

Rebekkah Barry (10)

All About Me

I love my Horrid Henry books,
I also love my dolls
But my most favourite things
Are my dressing up clothes.
I can change all my looks
From a princess in a castle
To a mermaid under the sea,
I can be a monkey up a tree
Or a baby on Mum's knee
Or I can be plain old me!

Lauren Parfit (8)

This Is Me!

Watching Mamma Mia and playing with my dog
And roasting a marshmallow on a log.
Washing my hair with Sunsilk shampoo
And going to parties and dressing up too.

Putting up my Christmas tree
And going on a shopping spree.
Christmas bells ringing and flashing lights
And nibbling on the German makerbites
Are also things I like to do.

Opening Christmas present and reading a good book
And helping my mum to cook
Listening to X Factor and Abba too
Are also things I like to do.

Chelsea Sacha Stagg (11)

Value Of Time

Time goes past
Time is something which does not last.
You cannot make time wait
Postponing time will make you late.
So say to yourself, 'I shall do it today.'
Don't keep work for some other day.
Stick to time every day
No matter what may come your way.

Mishika Mahendra Parwani (11)

Christmas Time

Nights are cold and dark
Snowing fast, snowing hard, snowing all around
We just know it's Christmas.

Shimmery snowflakes, glittering, falling down
Icicles melting, dripping, drip, dripping down
We already know it's Christmas.

Creep to bed, Christmas Eve
Mince pies and milk, left on the hearth
Go to sleep, Santa's here.

Wake up, it's Christmas Day
Open the present, which one's for me?
I've been good, can't you see?

Charlotte Spiller (11)

Reynaud

I'm a crafty fox
Cunning as can be
You can rely on me
To cause as much trouble as can be.
You will not see me crouch
Your chickens at night
I creep very silent to steal
As much as I can eat.
Catch me if you can
Before I go to earth
I'm a crafty fox
Can't you see?
Till the next time
Maybe!

Louise Jillan MacKinnon (8)

The Lough Neagh Weather

Sometimes the Lough that looms across the bay
Is often sailed by people once or twice a day.
But when it's cold and windy no one dares to say,
'Let's go out and sail in the deep dark Lough today.'
The roaring of the wind, the crashing of the waves
Then the calmness of the Lough suddenly came.

When it's wet and stormy I hear no one say,
'Let's go out and sail in the deep dark Lough today.'
Early in the morning the fishermen return
Singing the fishermen's song in the silence of the morning.

Soon it will be spring and all the birds will sing
And the storms will fade away
And the Lough Neagh fishermen
Can once again sail on the Lough another day.

Karen McAllister (10)

Snow

Snow is falling
A beautiful sight,
Snow is falling
It plays with the light.
Snow is falling
It plays its game,
Snow is falling
It makes all that is different look the same.
Snow is falling
Its source is the storm,
Snow is falling
It makes all conform.
Snow is falling
It blinds all who see,
Snow is falling
It hides you from me.
Snow is falling
From a sky of lead,
Snow is falling
On your head!

Cameron Harper (11)

My Mum

My mum looks like roses and she looks like sugar and sweet cakes
Also she looks like my brother
My mum goes to work to get us money but never catches a bus
My mum has got brown hair and dazzling green eyes
She likes big surprises
When she has a bath she goes red
But then goes to bed
And what she says is, 'Go to bed,' to me.

Gemma Mae Burke (7)

Christmas With My Family

Christmas Eve is very nice
Even though it's as cold as ice.
If we're lucky it will be white
Then we'll have to stay warm all night.
All my family come to eat
And then after dinner we'll get a treat.

One Christmas Day we get up early
My new doll's hair is very curly.
After we have opened presents
My mum then cooks the pheasants
We eat tea with all we treasure
Afterwards we eat dessert with pleasure
Christmas day was very fun
Now I'm sad that it's all done.

Bethany Hare (9)

Christmas

N ot long now
O nly weeks to go
V ery little time to pass
E veryone preparing
M any things to do
B usy, busy, busy
E veryone shopping
R emembering everything

D id you go to sleep early?
E ager to wake up
C hristmas morning is here
E veryone in town excited
M any presents to open
B illions of them
E veryone downstairs
R ipping them open!

J ust as Christmas is over
A nd all the snow is gone
N ew Year's Day has come
U ltra, ultra fun
A nd everyone cheering
R eally shouting out
Y et another year to come!

Sam Tait (9)

My Little Hamster

My little hamster
Is pretty and is cute,
He runs around everywhere
And climbs up on my foot.
He climbs upon his little wheel
And round and round he goes,
To where he thinks he's going
No one really knows.
He has his little hut
And there he's made his nest,
He curls into a little ball
And then he goes to rest
In his little home.
It's there he stores his food,
I love him so much
As a pet he's really good.

Jordane Julia Cummins (11)

I Remember The . . .

I remember the soft chocolate centre seeping out of the Christmas pudding.
I remember the glow of the fire's flames warming up my face,
The whistling whisper of the winter winds in my ear
And smelling my mum's perfume on her chest when I cuddle her.
I remember my mates joking to get the Jonas Brothers to play at my birthday disco
And pretending to ring them with their cousin's number.
I remember trying on my new school blazer for the first time,
Perfect fit I thought gladly.

Catherine Bradley (12)

Make-Up

M agical colours red, green and blue
A beautiful image staring at you
K eep your hands off - you know it's mine
E veryone needs it - to stay looking fine

U p in my bedroom or chilling with friends
P eople all around me and make-up never ends.

Georgina Bennett (12)

A Girl With Many Talents

To those who are given
Much is expected.
That's what people say
For those must be respected.

Dancing and singing
Colouring and books
Riding on their bike
Not caring about their looks.

Ice skating and story writing
Camping and playing hockey.
Training day and night
Ignoring those who are cocky.

Listening to music and singing along
Wearing pretty clothes and rings.
Happy days when cousins come to stay
These are a few of my favourite things.

Annabelle Fowler (10)

Senses

Sour or salty, bitter or sweet, I am your taste buddy whenever you eat.
I can help so very much if you need the sense of touch.
If you need help day or night, I will help you with your sense of sight.
I send messages brain to ear, if there is a sound I'll help you to hear.
If it's pongy or smelly but you can't tell, I'll help with your sense of smell.

Georgie Hope Gregory (11)

Alone

As I sit at home, I feel so alone
Sometimes in the dark and cold I cry
Longing for lost loved ones to say hi.
But knowing that right by my side
My mother and my brother are there at those times.
So when you're feeling so alone
Sitting in the dark at home,
Turn to your family, they are always there
To love and support you and they always care.

Heather Clarke (12)

The Lady With Silver Hair

She touches the roses
And the petals fall to the ground.
She paints the water silver
But she doesn't make a sound.

The air has a outline of a body
The wind creates her hair,
She glides through the clouds
It's the lady with silver hair.

She sinks into your body
Making you shiver down your spine.
She breathes at the back of your neck
And tickles the toes of mine.

The air has an outline of a body
The wind creates her hair,
She glides through the clouds
It's the lady with silver hair.

She leaves the colour with her crayons
She colours your grass so white.
She makes music with her flute
And she says awake at night.

The air has an outline of a body
The wind creates her hair,
She glides through the clouds
It's the lady with silver hair.

The person that smiles at me
And cheers me up when I'm gloomy.
She takes me to her land of dreams
That's the lady with silver hair and me.

Thasin Choudhury (11)

Untitled

This cat's on my doorstep
I think he's here to stay.
I'm trying all my best
Just to scare him away.

The cat wasn't feeling good
He had a bit of a chill.
He couldn't stop shaking
I knew that he was ill.

His eyes were red and watery
His nose kept running too.
His cheeks were pale blue
And he frightened me too.

I took him to the vet
His nose was dripping wet.
I was trying all my best
Just to change his vest.

On the way back
He had an attack
Because while we were there
He saw a bear.

I brought him from the vet
He was very good.
I took him back to the house
He was as quiet as a mouse.

I fed him a bit of milk
That was very runny
And as he was drinking it
So I found it quite funny.

I've had lots of fun with this cat
And he likes sitting on the mat.
I think he's had lots of fun with me
Because I always give him tea.

Leah Rees (12)

A Hug From My Mum

A hug from my mum makes me cheerful when I'm glum
A hug from my mum helps me sort the problem when I know
                                                          I've been dumb.
Her hugs are so tight they help me sleep in the night.
Her hugs are so softening I feel like I'm in a pile of clothing.
When I fall in the dirt her hug heals the part that is hurt.
When I play my guitar her hug tells me I'm a star.
A huge from my mum before a cycle helps
Me go out for miles and her replies will be smiles
And that's why I love a hug from my mum.

Dylan Chambers (7)

Endangered

Avec fur or non-furry
    But certainly ought to worry
    'Cause they might be factorised
    And wolfed down with a curry?
They dawdle around so free
    Though living, but unable to foresee
    That spur of the moment
    Within which a metallic metal
    Or an axe non-brittle
    Might make them life free.
Whilst they hunt indispensable prey
    Are *themselves* bruised to grey
    For the malicious sapiens' greed
    In whose collusion they seldom lay.
    We know they're critical
    But *they* are carefree!
    Exotic to the giant expeditions
    Into their territory.
So from vulnerable they might slither
    Into the endangered category
    And if these incessant killings
    Continue for jewel and billings
    Their endurance might be immense worry.
The 'might' isn't the uncertain
    'Cause the truth's not behind the veil
    That time isn't long away
    When there fervent bruises won't heal.

Sambhav Gupta

Shimmering - Haiku

Snowflakes fall softly
Drifting downwards to the ground
They melt on my tongue.

Umara Iqbal (8)

Fear

Fear, stop creeping through my window
In the middle of the night.
Fear, stop hiding under my pillows
Waiting to give me a fright.
Fear, stop hiding in my wardrobe
Waiting to jump out and shout.
Fear, stop trying to scare me because
I'm not scared anymore!

Uzo Anthony-Uzoeto (10)

The Wedding

When I was at a wedding
I stole the bride's ring
But when she looked for it
She found a funny thing.

The funny thing chased her
Until her dress fell off
She fell over a chair
Then she heard a strange cough.

The cough was her husband
She really didn't know why
The wedding hadn't started yet
But when it did she began to cry.

She still hadn't found her ring
But she really didn't care
They had a lovely honeymoon
Then she lost all her hair!

Holly Louise Longthorn (9)

Dazzling Fireworks

Fireworks, fireworks they fly in the sky,
Fireworks, fireworks they dance so high!
Rocket, rockets, they are such fun,
They set off like a blazing gun!
Bonfire is everyone desire,
Sparkles, sparklers in the air
You don't touch, you don't dare!
Please join in our firework fun
But remember to take lots of care!

Jacob Rimmer (8)

Footsteps

Footsteps in the rain, faintly you hear them
They've always been there nothing you couldn't handle

Pulse races due to irrationality and human instinct
Breath shortens, this is your reaction

Reaction to little situations, exaggerated by paranoia
And society's threat, seed up

Now you're worried, now after your imagination
Has made its possibilities influenced by media and filtered, processed news

We read lies, believe them and model our lives around them,
　　　　　　　　　　　　　　　　　commonsense is scarce
Nuclear weapons and terrorism are apparently not, we walk in
　　　　　　　　　　　　　　　　　shadows of stupidity

Minds becoming even more fragile with every headline recession dawns over innocent thoughts
Slowing down isn't a bad option, just a careless one

Who dares to look back, whose mind allows them
The injection of false panic has rendered us all collateral damage

Slaves to the system, we walk, our quiet innocent lives were a delusion
Give up this fantasy and slow down or create a supplement and risk

Those footsteps gain, they've lacked awareness
Sole consideration for yourself has accumulated a generation of doubt

You can run but these footsteps are faster
So hide in your self pity and surrender to the nearing troubles
Perseverance is challenging in the twilight, we have but moments to make amends
Presuming we are not past the point of no return time will tell, so we wait

Our inconsiderate last minute action will dissipate in vain
For our attempts are patronised by our problems

These skies reflect out low spirits, exhibit our uncivilised society
Packed with sin and immorality, our expectations are pathetic

This is not living, this is not fun, this is not being dealt with
Have our bodies become immune to these footsteps,
Are we incapable of realisation?

Robert Staines (13)

Christmas Day

Here go the days
To Christmas Day
And the boys go home
Oh I'll miss my mates
But I can't wait
For Christmas and presents and all
In the dark night
With the moon in sight
I hear a noise downstairs
I creep down the stairs
But only to see
Rudolph eating biscuits with glee.

Mikhail Adetunji (7)

I Am A Peasant

I am a peasant
Poor as can be,
We are given some land
From the aristocracy.
It's not much land
Barely any,
We have to work for them
Rarely earning a penny.
My clothes are dirty
Torn and rough,
To be a peasant
You have to be tough.
If you are ill
You may not survive
Help save him please
A mother cries.
We usually eat porridge
A rather dreadful dish,
If only we had something nice to eat
I really do wish.
I dream of a time
When the harvest is good,
I am treated fairly
And get paid what I should.
I am a peasant
Poor as can be,
My clothes are dirty
I want to be free.

Anna Everest (12)

My Favourite Things

In western lands beneath the sun
The flowers may rise in spring
The trees may bud, the waters run
The many finches sing or there may be
This cloudless night as swaying beeches bear
The eleven stars as jewels white, amid and their branching hair

Though here at journeys end, I lie in darkness buried deep
Beyond all towers strong or high, beyond all mountains steep
Above all shadows rides the sun and stars forever dwell
I will not say the day is done, nor bid the stars farewell.

Ben Cross (11)

A Hungry Shark

The shark he has a terrible grin
With his lethal fin
Swimming through the sea
Looking for me!

Eating the fish
His perfect dish
Going in ease
Paying no fees.

Having no mercy
Coming from New Jersey
Hiding when he comes
Biting thumbs.

His teeth as sharp as a knife
Going near him will risk your life.
Getting his fork
His diet without pork.

Ziad Al-Dujaili (8)

Take Me To The Moon

We flew on a shooting star, to the moon we shot.
The we stopped to watch the world go by
Gracefully the stars danced across the night sky
Then I found I was still in bed.

Now it's bedtime again, I wonder where we will go?
I wonder if we will go to Venus or Pluto?
I feel tonight I will meet an alien called Wiggle
But the star did not, so it flew in a squiggle.

Then we ate space biscuits on board
After we flew around the world.
And we met an alien called Afford
I wonder where I'll go tomorrow night?

Rhiannon Wilkins (9)

Seasons

Sunshine on sunny days
Raindrops on my window
The misty moon in the sky
The odd spaceship floating by
Fairy dells and chestnut shells
Rainbows up above
Frost pattern on the windowpane
And snowmen in the garden
Picking apples
Rustling leaves
The scabs from climbing trees
Mushrooms great and small
Watching rabbits crossing fields
The flowers in the hedgerows
Waiting to be picked.

Alice Marriott (9)

Night

The clock struck twelve
Magic is about.
Around every corner
I hear a magical sound.

I sit by my window
And to my surprise
A whole new world
Opens in front of my eyes.

High above in the dark blue sky
Stars twinkle and shine out bright.
Down below in the long green grass
Wonderful animals crawl and dance!

I look around in wonder
At all these fantastic sights
Night is truly magic
I hate to say, 'Night night!'

Racquel Quinn (8)

What Am I?

Fins, pointy poised, deadly
Gills long, breathing madly
Eyes bright, scanning horribly
Teeth sharp, grinning hatefully
Can you guess?
Yes, a shark!

Molly McKenna (9)

I Like The Weather Now

A row of trees
Swaying in the breeze,
While watching out for rain.
All of them are bare
They're leaving their leaves behind.

Frosty grass
Green no more,
All white now
As it grows and grows
As it did before.

Crispy little leaves
Wave goodbye
As they leave their trees.
Although they are old
They soon will get another life!

Playtimes not as they used to be,
Playground frosty and cold.
Not allowed at school without a jacket.
No more ice cream either!
Have to sit next to the fire with your family!

Aina Ahmed (10)

What A Wonderful Christmas

Christmas is a lovely time
Yummy pudding can be fine.
Christmas trees are shining bright
Hope Santa has a lovely flight.
Christmas cracker are going *bang!*
Down the road the choir sang.
Presents under the Christmas tree
In the garden the children go *yippee!*
Snow comes down from the sky
Sun comes up, snow says goodbye.

Paige Murphy (9)

Memories

Memories to cherish
Memories to share
Memories to keep
Memories of my childhood
As innocent as sweet
The foolishness and laughter
I still remember
A wonderful dream
Having a bowl of my favourite ice cream

Sitting and thinking of my favourite things
Like cupcakes and flowers
Tears of sadness and joy
Sharing a secret, shouting out loud
Lying out in the sun guessing shapes in the clouds.

Naila Ali (11)

My Family

Last night Mum got really mad
And threw a jam tart at my dad!
Dad lost his temper then with Mother
Threw one at her and hit my brother!
My brother thought it was my sister
But somehow missed her.
My sister she is only three
Hurled four at him and one at me!
I said I wouldn't stand for that
Aimed one at her and hit the cat.
The cat jumped up like he'd been shot
And landed in the baby's cot.
The baby quietly sucking his thumb
Then started howling for Mum.
A t which point Mum got really mad
And threw a Swiss roll at my dad!

Yusuf Mohamed Makaran (10)

Ten School Computers
(Inspired by 'Ten Naughty Schoolboys' by AA Milne)

Ten school computers all online,
One went down and then there were nine.

Nine school computers till my mate
Blew one up, and then there were eight.

Eight school computers but one was from Devon
And had to be returned, and then there were seven.

Seven school computers but one always sticks,
So that was no good and then there were six.

Six school computers but one belonged to Clive
And he took it home, and then there were five.

Five school computers but one fell on the floor,
And then it wouldn't work, and then there were four.

Four school computers but one's for a brass band
Then there were three.

Three school computers till someone spilt some glue
And then there were two.

Two school computers and one was left in the sun
And then there was one.

One school computer, children don't run
Bang, crash twinkle . . . and then there were none!

Sabeela Shamraiz (10)

World War

My arm hurts, 'Ow!'
The cold got me
No one to be friend thee
Love turning to hate

No one to love
Everyone goes as quickly as the wind, *whoosh*
Wise men, wise men
Are not expecting to be dead

Hatred as bitter as lemon
Heart can feel for completely nothing
Pain has overtaken thee
Furiously and painfully
Nothing is left in me

Thou shalt not turn to this
At all risk they will become more hurtful
Respect is not worthy of this terrifying heartache.

Iveren Yongo (13)

My Box

(Based on 'Magic Box' by Kit Wright)

I will put in my box . . .
The dancing china dragon breathing fiery flames,
The fresh scent of the most famous smell of the finest wine
And the smoothness of a baby's skin after being in the bath.

I will put in my box . . .
The quiet sound of a cat purring with joy,
Lollies as tasty as a rainbow,
Red like a rich ruby sparkling in the sun.

I will put in my box . . .
The hate of PE in school,
The love for my dog Tammy
And a memory of love.

My box is fashioned from red hearts of love,
Wishing stars, secret dreams and precious memories.

Alicia Roe (9)

There Was Once

There was once a little hurricane
She was called Katrina
But as she crossed the warm oceans
She became bigger and bigger and bigger
As she came to New Orleans
She was so big and strong
She killed thousands and thousands of people
She ruined the buildings
And flooded the streets
She made a big disaster
Everything happened
Because of global warming
And it will happen again and again and again
If we don't fix this major problem
Stop global warming
I say stop global warming
Or else it will happen again and again and again!

Joanna Elisabeth Lee (12)
Birralee International School, Norway

Polar Bear

My name is Polar Bear
And I'm swimming for my life
So by my side swims my wife
Then again
We are swimming for our lives
Our icy world is melting
And our paws are burning.

Conrad Johannes Bali (12)
Birralee International School, Norway

Can We Get Rid Of Global Warming?

Can we get rid of global warming?
Of course we can. But how?
Stop cutting trees and plant more and more.
Stop burning fuels and use renewable energy source.
Use pure fuels for cars and don't throw garbage on roads.
What if we don't stop global warming?
I think we will die! But how?
The ice caps on both Poles will melt
And the sea level will grow up
So there will be water everywhere.

Shreeram Ro Akerkar (12)
Birralee International School, Norway

What About Our Future?

Global warming
Deforestation, nature problems and animal extinction
Polar bear drowning and baby chicks starving
Glaciers melting
Our future is in danger
Tsunamis and hurricanes destroying our world
Why do we think recycling is hard?
Think of our future.

Rebecca Gjaetrvan Saether (12)
Birralee International School, Norway

Recycle!

If you don't recycle
There will be global warming.
If you don't recycle
Many animals will die.
If you don't recycle
There will be more hurricanes.
If you don't recycle
You damage the world.
If you don't recycle
We will all die.

Mats Langseth (12)
Birralee International School, Norway

Save The World

Today's the day we stop pollution
And people think it's a good solution
Racism has got to stop
Black or white it involves the cops
Recycling is helping as you can see
All animals and plants are friends with me.
Some people are rich some people are poor
Where money's concerned it's always war.
So now's the time to make it the same
Save the world from climate change.

Phoebe Miller (12)
Cardinal Allen School, Fleetwood

Eco

Eco-friendly is the game,
Eco-friendly we will gain.
Growing crops of fruit and veg
Corn and maize will raise their heads.
Keep the water in the well,
Use the rain as it will swell.
Compost this and compost that,
Don't put the goodies in the trash.
Keep walking is the game,
Keep the traffic off the lane.
So keep the air so clean and fresh,
So eco-ways are the best.

Sally Price (10)
Crossgates Primary School, Llandrindod Wells

Animals

A nimals need to be cared for
N uts are the favourite things for squirrels
I f everyone's like me they'll want to help animals
M ammals are like carnivores and herbivores
A nimals need to be protected
L ots of animals are in danger
S ome animals are nearly extinct.

Gareth Owen (9)
Crossgates Primary School, Llandrindod Wells

Recycle

R ecycle paper and plastic
E nvironment should be clean
C ontrol your rubbish
Y ou should respect the world
C an you help the environment?
L ights should be turned off
E nergy can be saved.

Morgan Margetts (9)
Crossgates Primary School, Llandrindod Wells

Recycle

R ubbish is horrible it's like dragon poo
E lectricity is polluting the planet
C utting down trees that give us oxygen
Y ou can make a difference recycling
C utting paper for no reason is wasting the trees
L andfill is coming from you putting rubbish in a normal bin
E arth is a special place!

Lauren Jones (8)
Crossgates Primary School, Llandrindod Wells

Animals

A little bit of help is what you need
N ormally we just like to feed
I think you'll want to help us
M ake the world go green for animals
A pples eat them up
L ike a pup
S o don't waste the world with rubbish use it!

Siobhan Margaret Patten (8)
Crossgates Primary School, Llandrindod Wells

Animals

There are lots of animals in the world
Lions, leopards and lizards,
Parrots, peacocks and pandas too.
I like these animals but do you?
I like the seagulls up in the sky
And the little baby birds starting to fly
I like these animals, but do you?

Carys Powell (8)
Crossgates Primary School, Llandrindod Wells

Rubbish

R ubbish kills animals
U nless you bin it
B ring your rubbish home
B in it when you can
I f you see people drop rubbish pick it up
S ave the animals
H elp keep the world green.

Ben Jackaman (9)
Crossgates Primary School, Llandrindod Wells

Health

H ealthy eating is the test
E ating apples is the best
A ll sorts of fruits are good for you
L ovely jubbly, the world can be healthy too
T hink about your diet
H ealthy foods are good for you.

Minnie Alder (8)
Crossgates Primary School, Llandrindod Wells

Earth

E arth is excellent
A pples and fruit are healthy
R ubbish wrecks your land
T he Earth will stay green if you clean
H ills are green, land is unclean.

Tom Dunt (8)
Crossgates Primary School, Llandrindod Wells

Earth

E co-friendly
A nimals are dying because we're not recycling
R ubbish wrecks our land
T he Earth will stay green if we clean
H ills are going and landfills keep coming.

William Dunt (8)
Crossgates Primary School, Llandrindod Wells

Eco, Eco

Eco, eco is the game
Recycle it, not bin it, that's the way!
Eco is the best way, save it, don't waste it
Eco, walk more, drive less
If you see litter on the floor, pick it up, that's the eco way!

Abraham Berriman (9)
Crossgates Primary School, Llandrindod Wells

Please Be Eco-Green

Please be eco-green
Mountains high will be seen
Bins are here for a reason
Flower are here every season
Open the gate
Be eco-great!
So *please,* be eco-green!

Emily Pugh (9)
Crossgates Primary School, Llandrindod Wells

Composting

C omposting peelings help the environment
O range peelings can be put in the compost bin
M any people in the world do this and you can too
P lease compost to help the world
O rdinary people around the world do this
S urely everyone can do it
T hink big with composting
I nventing new ways to help the environment
N anas, oranges, peeling and apple cores can be composted
G rowth of fruits makes the world a happier place.

Chloe Lisa Jones (9)
Crossgates Primary School, Llandrindod Wells

Environment

E veryone should help everything
N obody should hurt anything
V alleys hold cows that go moo!
I f I can help it so can you
R oaming birds fly free
O nly good people like it like you or me!
N ightingales sing with greatest of ease
M ajestic oaks and graceful yews
E vergreen trees grow by your shoes
N ever underestimate the power of nature
T each people it, don't save it till later!

Jessica Layton (9)
Crossgates Primary School, Llandrindod Wells

Eco Is The Best!

Eco, eco, eco, it is good for you and me
So help the world to stay green
Green is the colour we like to see
So walk around, it helps you and me
Don't throw away the things that can be recycled
Pick up things if they can hurt animals
So help the world to stay green
So go on go on, recycle what you can
Use as little petrol and diesel as you can
Eco is the best!

Josef Dunn (9)
Crossgates Primary School, Llandrindod Wells

In The Rainforest

In the rainforest there are dark corners
Scary animals crawl all around
Up above monkeys jump from tree to tree
Down below snakes slither under logs with parrots overhead
That is what goes on in the rainforest.

Tyler Owens (9)
Crossgates Primary School, Llandrindod Wells

Winter

Outside
Ice on the puddles
Frost on the trees
Sparkling ice on roads
Frosty roofs
Falling snow melting
Fields white with ice

Inside
Bright Christmas trees
Glowing baubles
Bits of wrapping paper on floor
Wet boots dirtying Mum's clean floor
Looking under the Christmas tree feeling what's in the presents.

Andrew Bowyer (9)
Longstone Primary School, Ahoghill

Winter

Outside
Ice skating on sparkling ice,
Sliding on the icy footpath.
Snuggling up in your warm coat,
Building a giant snowman and wrapping your scarf round him,
Feet crunching in the snow.

Inside
Warming your toes on the hot fire,
Snuggling up in your duvet.
Drinking luxury hot chocolate in your pyjamas,
Eating Christmas pudding and turkey,
Writing your Christmas cards at the kitchen table.

Tara McClure (9)
Longstone Primary School, Ahoghill

Winter

Outside
Icy roads on the way to school,
Frosty windows in the morning,
Bare black trees,
Fields covered in a white sheet,
Catching snowflakes.

Inside
Warm fires blazing keep you warm,
Christmas tree lights shining in the dark,
The smell of Christmas dinner,
Waiting for Santa to come!
Watching snowmen melt.

Hollie Dickey (9)
Longstone Primary School, Ahoghill

Winter

Outside
Ice skating on the sparkling ice,
Roofs covered with snow,
Stamping on the crunchy grass,
Trees shivering with white snow on them,
Cars sliding on icy roads.

Inside
Sitting beside a warm Christmassy fire,
Snuggling into your nice warm bed,
Drinking boiling hot coffee,
Getting into your nice warm pyjamas
Unwrapping presents, throwing paper all over the floor.

Jack McMillen (9)
Longstone Primary School, Ahoghill

Autumn - Haiku

Sparrows migrate south,
Over oceans deep and blue,
Warmer skies they seek.

Scott Harris (11)
Longstone Primary School, Ahoghill

Favourite Things

F lying high in an aeroplane
A t a friends to play all day
V ery good games in an old bunker
O ut secret little hideouts all over the place
U kraine and Germany, I love to travel
R eading gives a lot of fun
I love to go swimming in the pool
T eatime has come, I'm about to start
E ating a lovely fresh steak pie

T rying to get some models completed
H olidays are the best of all and
I love the summer!
N intendo and PlayStation are good pastimes
G oing home from school. There are
S ome of my favourite things.

Joshua McKay (11)
Longstone Primary School, Ahoghill

Winter

Outside
Roads glistening with ice
Robins hopping around on the ground looking for food
Tree branches covered with snow
The crunching of leaves where people walk
Trees are bare, no leaves.

Inside
Sitting down by the fire
Drinking hot tea, when it's cold
Butter melting on steamy hot toast
Christmas lights lighting up the room
Sitting down to a big Christmas dinner.

Jessica McMillen (11)
Longstone Primary School, Ahoghill

Winter

Outside
Watery sun melting the ice,
Robins looking for food,
Puddles frozen with ice,
Fields white with snow,
Bare trees with no leaves.

Inside
A warm open fire,
Hot chocolate warming you up inside,
A warm duvet to keep warm,
The Christmas tree lights twinkling,
Butter melting on warm toast.

Ruth McNeilly (11)
Longstone Primary School, Ahoghill

Winter

Winter outside
Snowy fields white with ice
Ice skater skating fast
Temperature drops to -3
Crunching feet on gravel
Building snowmen with frozen hands.

Winter indoors
Warm fires crackling along with crackers
People opening presents under the tree,
Eating Christmas dinner, waiting for dessert
Wet gloves, coats and jeans,
School children give out cards.

Christopher McKay (9)
Longstone Primary School, Ahoghill

Iraq

Why is this happening?
Why is it real?
What can we do
To stop this appeal?
What is going on in the world today?
Iraq, Iraq, Iraq.

All of the weapons
All of the dead
All of the injured
Lying in bed
What is going on in the world today?
Iraq, Iraq, Iraq.

All of the families
All of them sad
All of the funerals
All of them bad
What is going on in the world today?
Iraq, Iraq, Iraq.

When will it stop?
When will it end?
When will the break
In our world mend?
What is going on in the world today?
Iraq, Iraq, Iraq,
Iraq, Iraq, Iraq.

Rebecca Wilding (12)
Newall Green High School, Wythenshawe

Untitled

Litter, litter, litter, all over the streets
Is what you throw when you've eaten sweets.
Don't throw it on the floor put it in a bin or recycle it.
If you have got toys you don't want anymore,
Don't throw them away because someone else might want them.
When wearing clothes and you grow out of them,
Give them to the charity shops,
Someone else might want them.
Don't throw them away without thinking
Recycle them!

Natalie Greenwood (12)
Newall Green High School, Wythenshawe

Racism

Whether we're fat or thin
Black or white skin
God loves us all the same.
Whether we're dark or light
We play or we fight
God loves us all the same.

Simone Glindon (12)
Newall Green High School, Wythenshawe

Pollution

People walk onto the street
And look up to the sky,
Disgusting, smoky air
And black clouds pass you by.
You think to yourself, *why,*
Why did I help create
A colourless, smelly horrible world?

I mean, whose favourite colour is grey?
Do you want to live in a world
Which makes you run and hide?
A world with the climate so bad
It smells like something has died?
Well, you can change all this misery
But how do you stop the pollution?
You'll have to think long and hard
And you'll soon find the solution.
Stop people smoking and drive cars less
C'mon, guys, start being formal
Stop releasing gases into the air
And the world will return to normal.

Brooke Hirst (13)
Newall Green High School, Wythenshawe

Winter

I woke up this morning and it was winter.
It was very cold and snow was coming down.
I saw footsteps in the snow.
I could hear, *crunch, crunch, crunch* as people walked past my window.
I saw cars passing by slowly in the snow.
I felt happy when I saw the snow but it was cold!

Chloe Joyce (8)
Queensborough First School, Queensborough

Winter

I woke up this morning and it was winter.
It was quite cold and some schools were shut,
People were having snowball fights, I felt very happy.
I had a snowball fight with Chris, all I saw was fluffy white snow.
I heard a *scrunch* and a *crunch*
I made a snowman that's not finished.

Nicholas Post (7)
Queensborough First School, Queensborough

Winter

I woke up this morning and it was winter.
I looked out the window and I saw snow falling from the sky.
It looked like a big white blanket on the floor.
I heard people talking and having fun.
I heard a *crunch! Crunch! Crunch!*

Jack Batt
Queensborough First School, Queensborough

School Closed

I woke up this morning and I saw a white blanket.
Snowball fights, yeah!
School closed, yeah, yeah, yeah!
I was playing in snow
Come on guys, let's have a snow fight!
I am cold, unfair guys, stop guys!
Let's make a snowman.
Can I play in the snow please?
Snow angels, come on make them.
More snow yeah!

Ocea Ratcliff (7)
Queensborough First School, Queensborough

Green Space

Can't you see trees being lobbed?
Is that like what we feel when we are sick?
Seeing the dirty street.
Smelling the dirty street.
Makes most of the animals die.
So just think about
If you want to live more
You gotta let the green space live like us!
Because if it wasn't for the green
We wouldn't be here!
Please try every day,
Recycle and don't make pollution
If you want to live more.

Melissa Pontes (13)
Regent's Park School, Shirley

Spring Day

I see the trees swaying in the cold spring wind.
I hear the lovely birds singing in the swaying trees.
I touch the rough bark on the swaying trees.
I smell the scent of delicious onion rings.
I feel the warm sun beaming down on me.
I taste the lush grass rushing into my mouth.

Nathanial Humphries (10)
St Joseph's Catholic Primary School, Rugeley

A Spring Day

I see trees swaying in the wind and the fluffiness of the clouds in the blue
sky, home of the sun.
I hear cars moving in the distance, so noisy and loud.
I touch the roughness of the bark of the school tree.
I smell the newly mowed grass, so fresh and delightful and flowers blooming
in the sun.
I feel the smoothness of the carved wood of the table under the tree.

Keir John Scarlett (10)
St Joseph's Catholic Primary School, Rugeley

Curse

The mist creeps closer from the horizon
Edging its way towards the house in the marshes
The figures emerging from ghastly fog
Itching for revenge

The curse is upon them.
Their short time has drawn to an end
No more to look forward to but the
Sickly grip of death.

Those dark knights enter the house.
Silent
Panic rises in the house. The maids, the children,
Even the spiders scuttle from the horror that waits

The spirits are looking, searching
They know nothing can escape them
Not now.

The happy days are over, lost forever.
The curse is upon you, my friend
And there is nothing you can do.

Jack Seton (16)
The Rutland College, Oakham

Marching Tweeds

Shooters marching
In their tweed.
Dogs all barking
Off their lead.

Then they pause
For shortbread and soup.
Then off they go
Back to their troop.

Roast beef dinners
Yum for me!
Chit the chat
Then home for tea.

Snoozing by the fire
Just for a while.
Then wake up
In time for Countryfile.

Rachael Pick
The Rutland College, Oakham

Morning

Birdsong wakes me up
From a daze
My eyes burn with new light
Like a fire ablaze
For what was is gone
Sleep
Realisation dawns on me.
My mind refocus.
I stare up, to soporific to move.
My eye caught by beautiful crocuses.
Time for a shower as I'm now awake.
A lonely breakfast on a dazzling morn.
Even the prospect of work can be lifted high.
The sun beckons me out
So I follow its call.
I can only get so close.

Gary McDonald (16)
The Rutland College, Oakham

?

Every man walks a lonely road
But every road leads somewhere,
All in search to leave the truth lying bare,
Every tear of sadness or joy,
Every comment to spite or annoy.
We learn. Learn. Work and die.
I can't comply
So why are we here?
This place fills me with fear.

The tranquillity of solitude a joy for one
Or a depressing factor that's just begun.
The same sunset seen at the same time
But everyone's perception is different from mine.
We see things differently.
As we grow older, do things become clearer?
Do the answers come any nearer?

Men have been before and asked the same questions
But there's no answers, no suggestions,
So why are we here
And where do we go?
How do we find out?
When will we know?
Why are we here?
This place fills me with fear.

Rory McDade (10)
The Rutland College, Oakham

Tears In The Rain

Water slashes the air about me,
Diamond scratches on passing windowpanes.
Inside: warmth, comfort, love;
I stand alone in the cold,
Unable to reach what I seek.
Like my hopes, a channel of rain floats away,
Down the tarmac road.
The memories.
The lies.
Buckled, the grass is racked with pain,
Weeping dewdrops.
The ripples repel sympathy,
As do I.
Only in the rain am I safe,
For in the end
A raindrop is a tear.

Francesca Hepplewhite (16)
The Rutland College, Oakham

What Lucy Did

She thinks she is
A different class,
So she sits all day
By the looking-glass.

Emotions held
By safety pins,
Dorina's picture
Holds all your sins.
Pretentious views,
Boys in queues.
There she goes your
Human addiction.
You shed your skin like
A snake, on the
Dirty road to ambition.

Your eyes as black
And dark as tar,
That melt and burn
And drip and scar.
I'm the one waiting at the bar.

Stop looking at your silver spoon.
Your looks will fade too soon.

James Harrison (17)
The Rutland College, Oakham

The Night's Sky

to you there is
   no start
   no middle
   no end
      nor finish
cepheus you connect us
breathing chains over the world below
binding this world together
      regulus you reassure us
despite your midnight murmur
it takes skilled eyes to read your story
      etamin of endlessness
like life your treasure is hidden at
    times
and the descending world cannot see
        it still remains
dubhe   merak   poloris   pisces
   stars with precious glow
   remind us that you are not ours
you belong to the
    night
      the night's sky.

Rebecca Fisher (17)
The Rutland College, Oakham

The Hunt

My rosettes gleam with the morning sun,
    Watching, Waiting
I lie there in the bushes and the trees hiding,
    Watching, Waiting
The ice-cold lake luring unsuspecting prey,
    Watching, Waiting
My hunger heightened by no food for days,
    Watching, Waiting
I feel like a snake without any poison,
    Watching, Waiting
        I see you approaching, not knowing,
        I tense, my ears listening,
        I pounce, you see, but it is too late,
    Watching, Surviving.

Fiona Crew (17)
The Rutland College, Oakham

First Day

Walking through the open door,
Emotions running high.
Feeling stranded for evermore
With vultures in the sky.

I couldn't see a friendly face,
Though people were all around.
Escape had gone without a trace,
My feet were frozen to the ground.

A wave of fear and panic,
My body began to shake.
I started to feel quite sick,
Thinking of the friends I'd make.

As the crowd moved on
I followed in a trance.
People going, people gone,
Felt like a foreigner in France.

Walking to room N2
Long corridors like a maze.
No longer with the VC crew,
Back in the good old days.

My heart began to beat faster,
What weirdos would I meet?
Thinking about this disaster,
This was it, I took a seat.

Charlotte Bourne
The Rutland College, Oakham

Blessed

Divine is what you are,
Gorgeous is your body,
When we are apart
All I do is dream
Of the beauty,
The affection
That graces the earth
In you.

What have I done
To deserve someone like you?
A one off, a kind person,
Individual
Someone capable of so much.
Why choose me?
Blessed I must be
To be wanted
By an angel.

Tom Bell (16)
The Rutland College, Oakham

God's Regret

God created Man
As a part of nature not to
Take nature apart.

Tristan Robayo Price (11)
Trafalgar Junior School, Twickenham

Help Our Planet

Our planet is dying
So help it now
Recycle your cans
Walk, don't drive.

Week by week our planet rots away
So don't let it end this way
Your carbon footprint it's getting out of hand
We need to act to save our land.

William Nicholls (9)
Two Waters Primary School, Hemel Hempstead

Save

Reuse, recycle, reduce,
We need to save Earth now.
You need to listen to me
And I will tell you how.

Don't throw litter on the floor
Take it home with you.
Use the right recycling bins
That's all you have to do.

Walk instead of using cars
Reduce the nasty smell.
You'll not only save the planet
But you'll save money as well.
Save the planet.

Hasan Ali (9)
Two Waters Primary School, Hemel Hempstead

Change This World

What the world used to be
Is not what we now see
There were blue skies
These aren't lies
All this pollution
We need a solution
The rivers are flowing
As the wind's blowing
But global warming's going on
This is wrong and we all know
This really needs to stop.

Megan Stockford (9)
Two Waters Primary School, Hemel Hempstead

Recycle Now - Haiku

Litterbugs are bad
Dispose of your rubbish now
Pollution is bad.

The Earth will die soon
Pick up all your garbage now
The Earth is dying.

Different coloured
Bins, use for different things
Before the Earth dies.

Edward Langley (9)
Two Waters Primary School, Hemel Hempstead

Stop And Think

Let's all make a difference today,
Then we'll be happier in every way.
Save the animals, it is not fair
To show the world how much we care.
Global warming, to trees cut down,
Show a smile, not a frown.
Reduce, reuse, recycle,
Ride a bike or a unicycle.
To stop pollution
Let's find a solution.
Block greenhouse gases,
Or anything else that passes
To make a difference today!

Madeleine Greeves (10)
Two Waters Primary School, Hemel Hempstead

The Earth

The Earth is tipping upside down
And nothing is falling off the ground.
Animals are dying and time is flying
We need to act now or you will regret.
Go on, do it, fly up into space
You're leaving behind the human race.
So pick up the litter, you're doing the right thing.

Findlay Hardcastle (9)
Two Waters Primary School, Hemel Hempstead

Recycle

Our planet is doomed
But if we try we can save it
But if we don't it shall go *boom* and die.

So don't use cars, walk
Don't drop litter put it in a bin
Reduce landfills
Put out factories

Don't use boats and let peace come back.

Charles Monk (9)
Two Waters Primary School, Hemel Hempstead

The Eco War

Every day you cause more
By not walking to your door.
Instead you use the evil monster
Making pollution even stronger.
The ozone layer is breaking down
The Earth has on its unhappy frown.
But we can fight pollution by saying never
And always finding ways and working together.
So by recycling instead of in the bin
We can make sure we win.

Bryn Holmes (9)
Two Waters Primary School, Hemel Hempstead

Save It Today Or No Tomorrow

Why is this bad?
Because it is sad
The planet needs helping
All you can do is help us do it
If you don't care we will get nowhere.

We need to act now
Or we are going to go somehow
It needs to be saved with all our might
We can get it right!

Leah Howey (9)
Two Waters Primary School, Hemel Hempstead

Save The Planet

Please help the human race
Earth is a disgrace
Earth is ill
Let's save it with our will
Give it a rest
We will do our best
To save Planet Earth.

Please help the human race
This is our place
High pollution
Needs a resolution
Quick, before it's too late
Earth is in a state
Clean up the streets
As our hearts beat
Save Planet Earth!

Please help the human race
Save it at a fast pace
Your work will be worthwhile
It will go an extra mile
Save Planet Earth!

Charlotte Howey (9)
Two Waters Primary School, Hemel Hempstead

Don't Make A Mess

Why throw things in the street?
Put them in the bin and be neat.
You are being very lazy,
You are being very crazy.

This planet Earth is precious
And you know that it can't be replaced.
You need to act now
Or your home and my home will be erased!

I'm sure that you've got three recycle bins,
I'm sure that you've got lots of tins to throw away.

Think before you act
Are you doing the right thing?
We need to talk about it now!

Frankie Toseland (9)
Two Waters Primary School, Hemel Hempstead

Act Soon

Our world is dying
Day by day
Animals are disappearing
Some in a cage.

Who shall we blame?
Apart from ourselves
Pollution and war
Destroying our world.

We think about going to the moon
But when will we learn
To act soon?
We need to think about the human race
Will you?

Look at yourself
Change something
That's all we need to do
But who will?

Soon it should be you!

Aaron Wharfe (9)
Two Waters Primary School, Hemel Hempstead

Please

S ave our planet
A lways recycle
V alue everything
E arth is precious

T ime is crucial
H elp is needed now
E veryone must help

P lease don't ignore me
L ove everything if you don't
A dvertise, campaign
N ever be careless
E ffort is what is needed
T ime is running out.

William Howe (9)
Two Waters Primary School, Hemel Hempstead

Is This The End?

Pollution will be our evolution
If we don't act fast!
Recycle, reuse, reduce!

Our Earth will live longer in life
If we give the right advice
Our Earth will always last
We have got to act fast.

Be careful with your litter
Always use the correct bin
To stop the mess we're in
We need to make changes now!

Robbie McIvor (10)
Two Waters Primary School, Hemel Hempstead

Untitled

The Earth is hurt
Broken inside and outside
So we want to save the planet
The Earth is getting dirty.

Leon Axell-Gee (8)
Two Waters Primary School, Hemel Hempstead

Untitled

You've got to recycle or our world will be dead and we will be dead.
Don't drop litter, yuck!
Save the world.
Save us and bin the things that have to be binned and recycle please!
Save our world and save ourselves, recycle!

Myers Witter (7)
Two Waters Primary School, Hemel Hempstead

Litter Everywhere

Litter all around
So much to be found
Pick it off the ground.

So much litter all around
So much litter on the ground
So much litter to be found.

Litter will destroy the ground
Pick up what can be found
Litter everywhere!

Joseph Alexander Metcalf (7)
Two Waters Primary School, Hemel Hempstead

Litter

L ots of litter
I t's everywhere
T he Earth needs to clean up
T idy it up
E arth is dying
R ecycling.

Jack Cannings (7)
Two Waters Primary School, Hemel Hempstead

Litter Around The World

Litter on the ground
Help the world go round
By picking it up every day
Otherwise you won't be wise.
The litter will disintegrate into the soil
And the world will be smelly one day!

Lydia Victoria Bradley (8)
Two Waters Primary School, Hemel Hempstead

Recycling Is Fun

Litter on the ground
Don't throw it around
Recycle litter don't throw it away
The dirty litter please go away
Don't come again
Save me!

Jessica Finnamore (8)
Two Waters Primary School, Hemel Hempstead

Litter

L itter is horrible
I t's very smelly
T in cans can break
T ry to take them to the bin
E veryone should keep clean
R ecycle rubbish.

Jessica Pritchard (7)
Two Waters Primary School, Hemel Hempstead

Litter, Litter Everywhere

L itter, litter everywhere
I t's really smelly
T he Earth needs to recycle
T idy it up
E ven tiny bits of stuff
R ecycle.

Edward Shaw (7)
Two Waters Primary School, Hemel Hempstead

Untitled

World dying
Pollution everywhere
Disgusting pollution anywhere
Stop leaving rubbish unattended
Help, help to save the world
Stop pollution right now
Recycle, recycle
Now!

Matthew Say (7)
Two Waters Primary School, Hemel Hempstead

Save Our Planet

We need to save our planet today
Then we could all happily play.
Different coloured bins, green and black
Now it is the right time to act!

People talk about going to the moon
They don't care if our planet is doomed.
The universe can wait its turn
Planet Earth is my concern.

With every astronaut you send into the sky
You are killing this planet and letting it die.
Please save this planet, please save it now
All you need to do is know how!

Millie Shaw (10)
Two Waters Primary School, Hemel Hempstead

Why?

Why do we litter all over the street?
We must keep our world tidy and neat
What is the point in trapping those creatures
Underneath one of your beakers?

It makes me want to scream in disgust
Keep our planet clean we must.
If not, animals are getting extinct
People who litter, it's time to think!
Why?

Rory Howe (10)
Two Waters Primary School, Hemel Hempstead

Our Planet

Don't hurt animals
For their fur and tusks
It'll come back
To bite you later.

Reuse, recycle, reduce
Is what you need to do.
Always do what you can
To clean up our planet.

Our landfill sites
Are overflowing.
Clean up our planet
So there is no garbage.

Hannah Bartrip (10)
Two Waters Primary School, Hemel Hempstead

Oil

Oil rigs everywhere
Tipping oil bare
If one blows
No one knows
What'll happen next!

Look at Empress, Queen of the Sea
I wonder where she could be?
Quicker, quicker oil goes
Where to? No one knows.

We must act now
And not allow
The world to rid its oil.

Harry Owen (10)
Two Waters Primary School, Hemel Hempstead

Plundered Planet

Today our planet is alive
But what about tomorrow?
With the car fumes everywhere
It may destroy the ozone.

If we want to save it now
Stop with the engines.
All you need to know is how
To make the right decision.

There is a solution
To everything wrong.
Including the pollution
That could be life-long.

Hannah Baldwin (10)
Two Waters Primary School, Hemel Hempstead

Recycling

Recycle, recycle your rubbish
Tins, glass bottles and cans.
Port, wine and beer bottles
Save the environment.

Recycle, recycle your rubbish
Cardboard, packaging not to waste.
Put it in the green bin
And save the planet.

Recycle, recycle your rubbish
Fruit stones, peelings, where do they go?
In the compost, just like I do
This is our planet.

Our landfill sites have no more room
For cans, tins and paper.
Recycle the paper and save the trees
So this can be a better place to live.

Gail Miller (10)
Two Waters Primary School, Hemel Hempstead

The Cycle Rap

It's time to think,
It's time to change.
You got the power
To change the game!

Dirty rivers soaring into the sea
Sewage is coming after me.
Toxic waste will go away
But only if we recycle starting today!

Its time to think,
It's time to change.
You got the power
To change the game.

Take your bottles into the store
Get a refund, buy some more.
Give us a future where we share
Crystal-clear oceans, pure clean air.

Lucas Rogers (10) & Nicholas Roel-Adams (11)
Two Waters Primary School, Hemel Hempstead

Open Your Eyes

Why do we kill animals
Is it so much fun
To see pure innocence
Cower beneath a gun?

Pull that trigger
Put an end to a life.
Observe an animal
In pure and utter strife.

How would you like it
If they turned back?
Timid but savage
They ferociously attack.

Why we kill
It's hard to comprehend.
To this suffering
There is no end.

I believe the world can change
With a helping hand.
We can stop all this killing
And save the lush green land.

We humans are to blame
For the disaster being formed.
So save Planet Earth
You've already been warned.

Abigail Morris (11)
Two Waters Primary School, Hemel Hempstead

Animals In Agony

Stop hunting animals,
They're lovely living creatures.
If you watch them closely
You'll see their special features.

So please stop hunting animals,
They love you as much as I.
Some of them are endangered,
Some of them just cry.

So before you sit and watch TV
Think about the animals in need.
Why are you just sitting there?
Maybe it's because you just don't care.

Angela Chu (10)
Two Waters Primary School, Hemel Hempstead

Thinking Green

It's time to act; it's time to save,
You say it bold, you say it brave.
So you make the difference
You make the change.
Recycle your leftovers each day
So remember - reduce, reuse, recycle.

This is true, it's not a lie
But people hardly ever try.
So you use your voice
Because you have the choice.
So what do you say?
Let's all help today.

You each have three coloured bins
And you probably use up lots of tins.
So put it in the right place
And you can save the human race.
I'm telling you all of this
Because we're in a crisis!

Yasmine Hughes (10)
Two Waters Primary School, Hemel Hempstead

Hunting Me

I'm getting tired of people hunting me
But my heart is still beating.
My legs are still strong
But soon they will be weak.
I love my children as much as my soul.
My children are getting weaker day by day
Please help us and all the other tigers.

Amy Wordsworth (10)
Two Waters Primary School, Hemel Hempstead

Global Warming

Global warming, global warming,
Needs to end one day.
Global warming, global warming,
I wish it would go away.

Global warming, global warming,
Why aren't we all thinking?
Global warming, global warming,
Watch out, our world is sinking!

Global warming, global warming,
All we do is take, take and receive.
Global warming, global warming,
I want to live and breathe.

Global warming, global warming,
Eventually the world will die.
Global warming, global warming,
Come on, at least try!

George Morley (10)
Two Waters Primary School, Hemel Hempstead

Hunted!

I'm the hunted now
Because I have given up somehow.

My legs have stopped racing,
My heart has stopped beating,
My mind has stopped fighting,
My life has stopped before me.

I'm dying inside, I can't hide,
They'll put me to my death
Just for my skin you see.

I don't have a say in life, we all don't.
So cease! 21,000 of us killed a year!
The stress, fear, noise and constant chase.
Of all animals, Man is the cruel one
He is the only one that inflicts pain for the pleasure of doing it!
There is no way out,
I'm in the cross hairs of a scope-mounted rifle.
Help stop the fur trade going to the shops
You have a voice so make a choice.

Olivia Reeve (10)
Two Waters Primary School, Hemel Hempstead

My Protest

Litter, litter everywhere
Animals are suffering
The world is running out of room
Don't throw cans out of cars
Think about it
Think about it

Hedgehogs are getting stuck in your cans
Animals are dying
The RSPCA are always being called because of you
But because you care you can help

Think about it
Think about it
Help save Planet Earth
Please help now
I don't want to see a dirty planet and neither do you
Nobody has permission to litter
So why do you do it?
Think about it
Think about it
I don't want to see a dirty planet, do you?

Anna Bennett (10)
Two Waters Primary School, Hemel Hempstead

Hunting Animals

Hunting animals, hunting animals
Gives them a fright.
We've really got to do something
Before they bite.

Take care with all your might
Take care and they won't bite
Keeping them in cages,
It's just not right.

Don't wait for it to get worse
The animals are about to burst.

Jacob Jenkins (10)
Two Waters Primary School, Hemel Hempstead

Our Earth

L itter is a horrible thing, let's try and stop it working as a team
I need to stop the litter, I can't take it anymore
T ry to stop litter altogether
T ogether we can pick up litter, all as a group
E co-kids say litter is a disgrace for this big place
R evealing this mess to everyone, you will feel sad.

Paige Ann Ford (9)
Two Waters Primary School, Hemel Hempstead

World

Nature, nature, we love it so much, so why do we kill it every day?
Recycle, recycle, do it every day, never ever stop recycling.
Pollution, pollution, every day if you do it, you're leaving
                                        Mother Nature crying.
War, war, why do they do it? They're damaging our environment.
Cars, cars, why do they use them? They leave our Earth in pieces.
Whales and sharks, why do the kill them every day?
Trees, trees, stop cutting them down, recycle more.
Mother Nature can't take this anymore.
We can make a difference by doing one thing every day.
Healthy, healthy, keep our world healthy!

Tommy Walter (9)
Two Waters Primary School, Hemel Hempstead

Litter

People litter everywhere,
Others don't think it's fair.

More and more litter hits the floor,
Rubbish, rubbish get out the door!

Crisp packets and Coke cans
Should be put into rubbish vans.

Help to keep the Earth clean,
All those litterbugs are mean, mean, mean!

Fynn Archibald (9)
Two Waters Primary School, Hemel Hempstead

The Extinction Of The Animals

Save our animals,
We don't need to poach.
Save our animals
Even if a nuclear bomb doesn't kill a cockroach.

Save our animals,
Don't make poaching bands.
save our animals!
Rainforests are now inhospitable lands.

We need to save our animals
Whatever it takes.
We are letting fish die
In polluted lakes.

Save our animals
From fish to deer.
Save our animals
'Cause poachers are near.

Save our animals
We are cutting down their trees.
Save our animals
We are devastating the hives of bees.

Rutwik Mudholkar (8)
Two Waters Primary School, Hemel Hempstead

My Big Green Poem

Animals are dying out and that's what my poem's about
When was the last time you saw a shark, a polar bear, a tiger or even a skylark?
The planets full of wonderful things, creatures and plants and birds that sing.
The smallest character can make a huge difference
So if me, yourself and that guy work together we can too!

George Andrews (12)
Ysgol Uwchradd Llanfyllin, Powys

Mission Name: Planet Green

Our world has stopped being green
Because we've been so destructive and mean.
The fumes from our factories are melting the Poles
And that's making life difficult for those unlucky souls.
The rain hasn't stopped falling for the past year
And soon the world will know what they have to hear.
It's all down to global warming
And they're on their final warning.
That if they don't fix this mess
I'll try my very best
To make this world
A lean green growing machine.

Matt Wheeler (11)
Ysgol Uwchradd Llanfyllin, Powys

Bee Quick

You can make a difference
It's not really that hard
It's not like the dustbins are steel-barred.
So don't use cars, walk or take a bicycle
Remember to recycle, recycle, recycle, recycle.
Be green and don't be mean, save electric and be quick
Global warming is definitely not a trick.
Without trees there won't be bees or cheese
So save trees and the bees will come back
Petrol pollutes the world and the animals
So you won't have any nature channels.

Ryan Risdon (11)
Ysgol Uwchradd Llanfyllin, Powys

Save The World

Save the world, be a hero,
Get pollution rate down to zero!
Act now, act quick,
Try to save electric!
Hurry, hurry, in a flurry, you can help us all,
Recycle, walk to school, now you're on the ball.
Don't leave the tap on, or the TV
We can save energy, you and me.
Global warming is getting out of hand
Help me now I demand!
Water rising by the minute
Recycle your rubbish, don't just bin it!

Charlotte Turner (12)
Ysgol Uwchradd Llanfyllin, Powys

Global Warming

The world is changing fast
We have to act quick if we want it to last.
The BBC's lying
Wildlife is dying.
The Earth's happiness is all in the past
Us people do not have much time
How we're polluting it must be a crime!
Try not to use planes
And switch off the mains
Do this and we'll be just fine.

Shannon Pearce (11)
Ysgol Uwchradd Llanfyllin, Powys

Young Writers Information

We hope you have enjoyed reading this book - and that you will continue to enjoy it in the coming years.

If you like reading and writing poetry drop us a line, or give us a call, and we'll send you a free information pack.

Alternatively if you would like to order further copies of this book or any of our other titles, then please give us a call or log onto our website at www.youngwriters.co.uk

Young Writers Information
Remus House
Coltsfoot Drive
Peterborough
PE2 9JX
(01733) 890066